LOOKING BACK AT
WILMSLOW
Handforth, Styal & Alderley

Morris Garratt

Willow PUBLISHING

2

Willow Publishing 1983
Willow Cottage, 36 Moss Lane,
Timperley, Altrincham,
Cheshire, WA15 6SZ.

© Morris Garratt 1983

ISBN 0 946361 05 3

Printed by The Commercial
Centre Ltd., Clowes Street,
Hollinwood, Oldham.

Acknowledgements

The compilation of this book has been made possible by the co-operation of the following organisations and individuals who have kindly placed their photographs and knowledge at my disposal:

Cheshire Libraries and Museums, and Mr. Albert Hartley, Senior Librarian, and his staff at Wilmslow Library
Mr. David Sekers, Museum Director, and his staff at the Quarry Bank Mill Trust Ltd.
Mr. F. Willocks and Mr. H. Taylor, of Handforth
Mrs. Nancy Morton of Handforth, and the Manchester Studies Team, Manchester Polytechnic
Mr. F. Mitchell, of Gatley, and Mr. H. D. Boutell, of Kendal
Mr. F. E. Higginson, of Alderley
Mrs. G. Stark, of Cheadle Hulme
Miss V. Holden, of Over Peover, nr Chelford
Mr. H. Standring of Castleton, Rochdale
and Mr. W. Dumbell of Handforth
Mr. F. E. Heusel
Mr. A. Woodall
Studio Camm, Wilmslow
Berni Inns Ltd.
Boddington's Breweries Ltd.
Greenall Whitley & Co. Ltd.

Introduction

The name Wilmslow – as Wilmesloe, Wylmeslowe (1287), Willmeslawe (1513), and many other early spellings – can, strictly, only be applied to the church and churchyard; only in more comparatively recent times has the name been applied to the village which grew up in the townships of Bollin Fee and Pownall Fee. The ancient parish consisted of the four townships of Bollin Fee, which included Hough and Dean Row; Chorley, including the now separate civil parish of Alderley Edge; Pownall Fee, comprising Stanilands, Morley and Styal; and Fulshaw. Handforth, as Handforth-cum-Bosden, was a township within the parish of Cheadle, and was not added to the Wilmslow Urban District until 1936, after having been administered since the turn of the century by the Handforth Urban District Council.

This selection of photographs attempts to portray something of the character of an area which, over the last two hundred years, has passed from being a predominantly agricultural landscape, through a period of industrial activity – the Gregs at Styal, Symonds, Cunliffe & Co. at Handforth, and textiles (cotton, silk and fustian cutting) at Wilmslow itself – to its present role as commuter country, not only for Stockport and Manchester, but also for London.

M.G.
October 1983

Contents

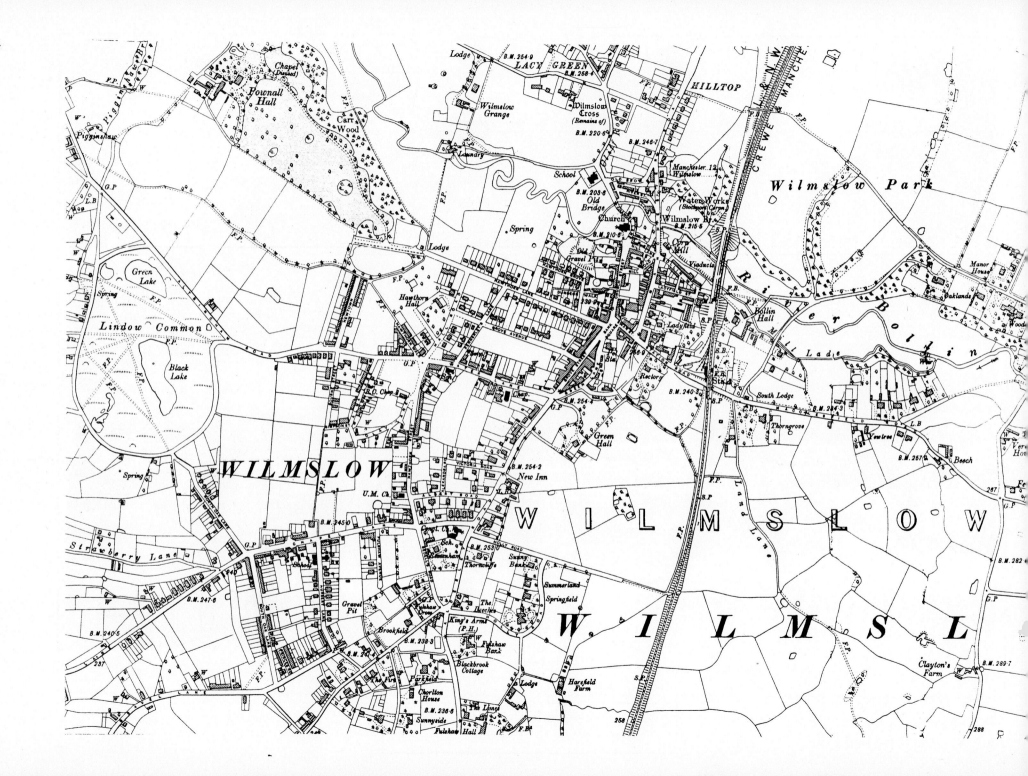

(Opposite page): 1907 map.

Bank Square, c.1920. *(right)*

In the succeeding 60 years perhaps the greatest
changes have been in Church Street, which leads
to the Parish Church. The gas works has gone,
and for some time the site was used by the North
Western Road Car Company as its Wilmslow
depot. The Vine Inn and Ring O'Bells public
houses have also gone, and the George and
Dragon now has a properly laid out car park.
Office buildings cover the gas works/bus station
site. On the right-hand side of Church Street a
supermarket is under construction on the site of the
market, and opened September, 1983.
The Catholic Church in Green Lane (bottom,
centre) dates from 1913. Grove Street runs to the
bottom left of the photograph, with Swan Street
going to the right of the photograph.

Wilmslow Station c.1890

The railway from Stockport to Sandbach opened on 10th May, 1842; the station buildings, seen here, disappeared and were re-built when the Styal line was constructed (Wilmslow to Slade Lane Junction). It opened to passenger traffic on 1st May, 1909 (goods traffic began on 8th February). The original two platforms were enlarged to four, and a new viaduct, parallel to the existing one, was built. The extra platforms were built on the site of the goods and coal yard on the western side of the station; the coal yard was a depot for Lord Vernon's Poynton and Worth Collieries.

PUBLIC WEIGHING MACHINE.

HERBERT ORAM

Coal and Coke Merchant,

Station Road, WILMSLOW.

Orders by Post
will receive
prompt attention.

BEST REAL OLD LANCASHIRE &
STAFFORDSHIRE COALS.

Office Hours: 8 a.m. to 8-30 p.m.

Saturdays, 2 o'clock.

HOUSE COAL

1902 advertisements

BURNS & RIDGWAY,

CONTRACTORS.

Coal, Coke, Lime and Gravel.

Also BUILDERS' MERCHANTS.

Estimates free for Slating, Sewering, Flagging, Paving,
Asphalting, Concreting, Gravelling and General Repairs
to Property.

Depôt: ALDERLEY EDGE & WILMSLOW

**Railway workers at Wilmslow station,
c.1890.**

They had to scythe the grass and generally keep
the railway embankment tidy – and all for 15/-
(75p) per week.

Mills on the River Bollin.

By 1800 a number of small cotton and silk mills had appeared in Wilmslow, using as a power source the waters of the River Bollin. In 1811 Samuel Crompton found that at Wilmslow there were 3 mills using jennies, with a total number of 7,440 spindles. This one (right) was originally a cotton mill, and was powered by an undershot wheel. Situated in the Carrs, 'a short distance west from the Church' (Bagshaw's *Directory of Cheshire*, 1850), it was later worked by Charles Barber of Macclesfield for throwing silk; indeed, it was popularly known as Barber's Mill (he rented it from the Bower family), or as the old Carr Silk Mill. According to Andrew Pearson, in later years it had been used for fustian cutting. It was destroyed by fire on 4th October 1923 while being used for storing gelatine; before that it had been used as a laundry, as the photograph shows.

The mill-keeper's cottage and the remains of the weir which controlled the Bollin, have also gone although traces of them can still be seen. The mill and cottage were on the northern bank of the river.

The 'Old Rectory'. *(below)*

It was built in 1778 by Rector Edward Beresford. In a letter to the Bishop of Chester, 6th April 1778, he says that 'the parsonage house is quite new, strongly built with double walls and perfectly well finished' though the outhouses were not. The previous Rectory, on the same site, had been 'in such bad condition as to make it necessary to pull it quite down and to build an entire new house'. This was the Rectory which had been besieged by Parliamentary forces commanded by Colonel Duckenfield during the Civil War, in which one or two of Rector Thomas Wright's servants had been killed. This earlier Rectory had 21 rooms and a gatehouse, enclosing a courtyard. Beresford's Rectory was still a substantial, if smaller, house, and with its gardens occupied some two acres. The construction of the by-pass in the 1930s took away part of the gardens. It has recently been restored and is now used as offices by a well-known Bank.

The Rectory. *(right)*

The story of Wilmslow's Rectories is somewhat complex. The earliest, Medieval, Rectory is thought to have been near the west end of the Church, on an area now covered by part of the churchyard. Other photographs of this house in Chancel Lane taken around 1900 show that it was the home of Daniel Sumner, boot and shoe maker; but there are indications that it may have been a former Rectory. 'There are remains of an old buttery, etc; all the tokens of a house of some pretensions'. So wrote the historian Earwaker, and it may be that this house is the Rectory of Henry Trafford (Rector 1542–1591), whose house had a hall, kitchen and buttery.

Water Lane and Grove Street c.1930. *(below)*

This is one of the more recent photographs in the book, but even here change has taken place. The stonemason's yard on the corner of Water Lane and Grove Street, has been replaced by shops, but the black and white building on the left still remains. All this side of the road is now given over to commerce. One wonders if the name of the road is indicative of its state under foot in times past, having regard to its proximity to the former extent of Lindow Common!

Wilmslow c.1920. *(above)*

This aerial view shows how the massive arches of the two viaducts dwarf the houses in Ladyfield Street and Bollin Walk. Prominent buildings on Station Road are the Railway Hotel (nearer the station) and the Wilmslow Picture Palace Co. Ltd. In the foreground is the Rectory in its extensive grounds.

Wilmslow Council School, Wycliffe Avenue (off Water Lane). *(below)*

This was officially opened on Tuesday August 2nd, 1910, by Mr. E. G. Leycester J.P., Chairman of the Administrative sub-committee for Education for the Knutsford and Wilmslow district, Cheshire County Council. The architect was Mr. H. H. Brown. The school was built to replace other schools suffering from overcrowding. This is the Infant Department, with the entrance for the boys to the left, and the girls to the right. It has now been demolished, to make way for housing development.

Sunny Bank Ladies' College *(right)*

The College was established in 1850.

A-BIG RECORD.

SALES JUNE 1859 to DEC 1909 AMOUNTED TO	£	10,627,795	15	11
HAVE PAID IN TO THE SOCIETY	£	872,801	1	1
HAVE HAD INTEREST CREDITED	£	229,015	13	4
HAVE HAD DIVIDEND CREDITED	£	974,274	2	4
WITHDRAWALS HAVE BEEN	£	1,842,486	1	10
TO MEMBERS CREDIT DEC 1909	£	223,826	18	4
THESE FIGURES WILL SHOW THAT MEMBERS HAVE PAID IN	£	872,801	1	1
HAVE WITHDRAWN	£	1,842,486	1	10
AND HAVE STILL REMAINING	£	223,826	18	4

Wilmslow Carnival.

The first Carnival was in 1909 and was organised by the Wilmslow Tradesmen's Association and the united Friendly Societies. The event was seen as a revival of the old Wakes' procession 'with a happy distinction. All the coarser features were eliminated . . .'. The proceeds of that first Carnival were in aid of a fund to provide a horse ambulance for the village.

The advertisement for the second Carnival, in 1910, held on Wakes Thursday, September 8th, speaks of two grand processions, one at 2.30, and an illuminated one at 7.30, with competitions for Historic Characters, Tableaux, Decorated Turnouts, and other attractions. The Carnival would be 'an enormous attraction on Mr. Paulden's Field on Holly Road'. There were Morris Dancers, Garland Dancers, and three bands, with a large bonfire, fireworks and dancing. 'Ten hours continuous entertainment' opened at 1.15; admission 4d, children half-price. We see here two contrasting floats.

At that first Carnival, the Morris Dancers had been 'imported' from Stockport. For the 1910 Carnival a local team was trained by Miss Warrington of Macclesfield (seen in the picture). The dresses, made by the Ladies of the Carnival Committee, were pale blue with black points.

Church Street.

A century ago Church Street was the principal shopping street, Grove Street then still being largely undeveloped. In 1851, 21 of the 36 shops in the central area were here. This was part of the original route from Wilmslow to Manchester (via Lacey Green) before the coming of the turnpike road, and echoed to the sound of the mail coach calling at the Ring O'Bells, the tall light-coloured building in the photograph. 'Chucky' Pearce used to sleep in the stables; he had a pony and trap. The village pump, seen in the photograph, (left), was demolished in 1908, and behind it can be seen the earlier Rectory protruding into Chancel Lane.

The market used to be held outside the church gate, at the bottom of Church Street, and is seen here (below) in a scene from the 1940s.

Methodist Chapel, Water Lane. *(left)*

'A Bit of Old Wilmslow' it certainly is, or rather, was; for this is the old Methodist Chapel in Water Lane, believed to have been founded in 1798, but known to have been in operation in 1800. The site is now occupied by Messrs Reda Ltd. The area was also known as 'Little Venice' but why this was so is not clear.

Cottages, Chancel Lane. *(below)*

Another 'Bit of Old Wilmslow' this time clearly showing the line of cottages on Chancel Lane opposite the Parish Church, and now the site of the Memorial Garden. The rear of the earlier Rectory may be seen to the left of the large house in the centre.

The old Police Station in Swan Street, c.1920. *(left)*

The site is now occupied by Lloyd's Bank. In 1915 the local police force consisted of an Inspector, George Gibbons, a sergeant, an acting sergeant and seven constables.

Swan Street, c.1890, looking towards Bank Square. *(above)*

Church Street goes off to the right, by Hopley's shop, and Manchester Road (constructed in 1775 as the turnpike road) is to the right foreground. The Swan Hotel, on the left, is an old coaching inn, and dates from before 1821.

Wilmslow Carnival, 1913.

The fifth Carnival was held on Wakes Thursday, September 4th. The President was Sir William Cobbett. The Grand Procession began at 2 o'clock; after leaving Mr. Paulden's Field on Holly Road, the route was: Alderley Road (Chapel Lane end), Grove Street, Swan Street, Manchester Road, Mill Road, Church Street, Hawthorn Lane, Kennerley Lane, Water Lane, Hawthorn Street, Chapel Lane, and back to the Field. Mr. Flitcroft, whose entry partly obscures the cinema poster, won 3rd Prize in the Tradesman's Turnout (Light) class. The Public Hall Picture House included 'Dora Thorne' in its programme, in addition to 'His Undesirable Relatives', a film which was 'beyond doubt one of the finest comedies yet seen in the district'. The object of this Carnival was the provision of a number of seats for Lindow Common. Two were subsequently donated by Miss Ingleby of 'Springfield' (via the Carnival Committee); shortly afterwards, the Committee provided 7 seats, supplied by Mr. C. Bilsborough, each bearing a plate inscribed 'Carnival 1913'.

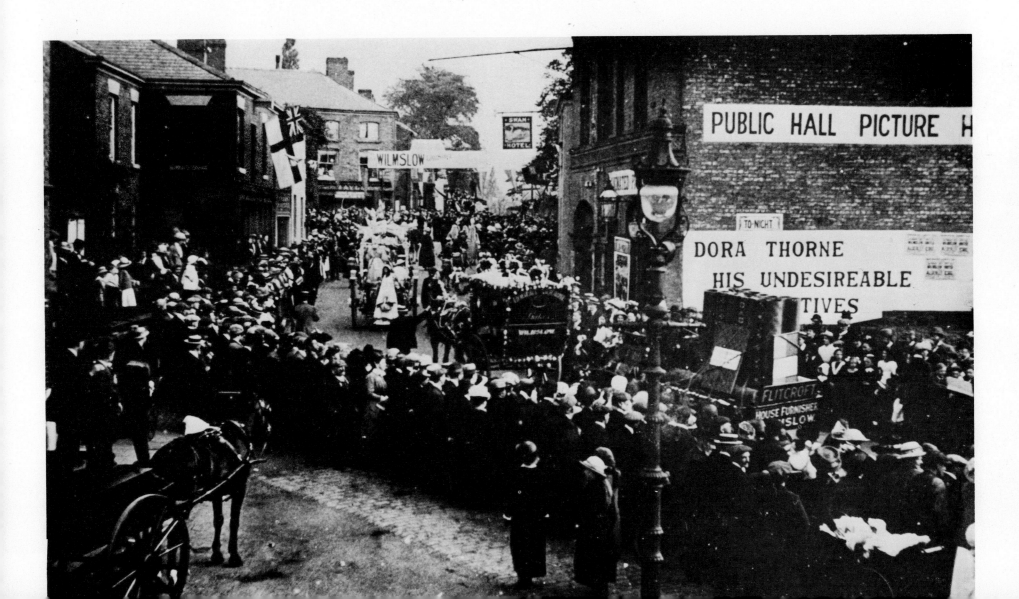

The River Bollin and Wilmslow Corn Mill

An interesting view, probably taken from the railway viaduct, and dating sometime before 1897. The River Bollin meanders across the foreground, with Wilmslow corn mill (now part of Messrs. Gibson's) in the centre.

Hawthorn. *(below)*

'Harethorn', was one of the lands which the Fitton family acquired from Matthew of Fulshaw, c.1220. In 1606 Henry Pownall sold the estate to John Latham of Irlam (d.1622). The Lathams held the estate until 1695, when it was sold to John Leigh. He demolished the existing hall and built the present one in 1698. After being in the ownership of the Bowers, the Hall became a boarding school in 1835. This school was acquired in 1843 by Thomas Somerville, and run by him for 40 years. In 1874 it was described as 'a classical, commercial and mathematical academy'. The Census Returns (1851) reveal that there were 24 boarders, including one from Spain and one from Greece. The Hall is now used as commercial offices.

Pownall Hall. *(above)*

Today it is a private school, but it was formerly a private residence. Mr. James Pownall bought the old hall about 1830 and largely re-built it as we see it today; it stands on the site of the ancient seat of the Newtons. Towards the end of the last century the estate was purchased by Henry Boddington J.P., who gathered together in the reconstructed interior of the Hall, 'so rich in heraldry and decorative work', a collection of works of art and musical instruments of past centuries.

Chapel Lane. *(above)*

As its former name of Mobberley Lane implies, Chapel Lane was once the main route from Wilmslow to Mobberley. It is here seen looking east, towards Alderley Road, from its junction with Hawthorn Street.

Hawthorn Street. *(opposite page)*

It was formerly called Pepper Street, and before that it was Lindow Side, a very descriptive name, for in the 18th century that is precisely where it ran – at the side of Lindow Common (towards Hawthorn Hall), which at that time had Hawthorn Street and Water Lane at its eastern boundary. These two views of the Street both date from c.1890, and look towards Altrincham Road. In the photograph the houses in the distance on the left are at the corner of Hawthorn Terrace, with 'The Hawthorns' replacing the cottage on the right. The photograph above shows the junction with Albert Road (on the right); on the left, in place of the cottages, are Chapel Court and Pepper Court.

The Railway Hotel, Station Road, c.1900. *(left)*

It was built, by 1860, by William Warham, after whom Warham Street is named. He had previously been at the Ring O'Bells, and remained at the Railway Hotel for about 20 years.

Station Road, c.1900. *(below)*

No traffic problems here! We are looking along Station Road around the turn of the century. The horse and cart is emerging into Station Road from Manchester Road. The three-storeyed building, now with shops on the ground floor, still remains, as does the black and white one; this stands on the site of a house granted by Sir Humphrey de Trafford in 1741 for use as a school. The wall (left) encloses the Rectory's grounds.

The Blue Bell Inn.

It is near Finney Green, and was first listed in directories in 1838, when it probably looked as it appears here. The licencee was William Cooper. It is not listed by name in either the 1851 or 1871 Census Returns, but does appear in 1861! The present building is the third on the site, replacing an earlier brick building which had itself replaced the one shown in the picture.

The New Inn, Alderley Road, c.1930.

Manchester Directories describing Messrs A. F. Holden & Co. Ltd. as motor coach proprietors and furniture removers are inaccurate. A descendant of Mr. Holden tells me that they were never motor coach proprietors. Arthur F. Holden, of Holmes Chapel, was a businessman whose hobby was 'spanking through the Cheshire lanes' with his own four-in-hand. He was a regular attender as shows and race meetings with his own team of black hackneys. A contemporary newspaper describes Mr. Holden as having 'one of only probably a dozen privately-owned coaching teams in Britain'. This photograph shows Mr. Holden outside the New Inn which has, incidentally, seen change since this photograph was taken!

Fulshaw Cross, c.1910.

It is perhaps difficult to believe that a quiet scene such as we have here could, some seventy years later, be transformed into the busy traffic roundabout we know today. In previous photographs, the only transport seen has been the horse; here we have a bicycle! The cottage (left) still remains, as do the grounds of 'Remenham', now a Cheshire County Council District Office, but formerly the home of Alexander Bedell, after whom Bedells Lane is named; the grounds are much cut back at this point. The King's Arms, built by Thomas Blower, a plumber and glazier, about 1830, has since been re-built. The Cross, or what remains of it, may be seen near to the Bedells Lane exit from the roundabout.

Parsonage Green, c.1880. *(right)*

The evidence from maps suggests that Parsonage Green may have originated as a separate hamlet. With its old houses, it was swept away in the 1930s to make way for the by-pass, but its name was retained. Then, as now, it stretched from Green Lane to Swan Street, at its junction with Manchester Road, and passed the extensive grounds of the Rectory – perhaps it is this juxtaposition which is reflected in its name. To judge from the photograph, it was anything but green, and the condition of the road left much to be desired. The building on the left was the old Liberal Club.

The Workhouse, Altrincham Road. *(left)*

The Deed appointing the Lindow Workhouse Trust is dated October 13th, 1772, and among the list of the first Trustees, all of whom had to be freeholders to the value of £30 per annum, we find the Rev. Edward Beresford, Clerk, Rector of the Parish Church of Wilmslow, in the County of Chester; Hugh Worthington, tanner; Samuel Finney; Thomas Stanley, baronet, and Ralph Bower. The Workhouse, seen here, was on Altrincham Road; the site is now occupied by Gorsey Bank School. When it closed as a Workhouse is not known, but as Wilmslow was in the Altrincham Union, it may have closed some time after 1834; certainly by the 1850s and 1860s it was being used as a farmhouse.

Station Road and Swan Street. *(left)*

After crossing the River Bollin, Manchester Road climbs the hill to its junction with Station Road (left) and Swan Street (right). The construction of the much-needed by-pass, in the 1930s, swept away the shops, and Back Swan Street, the narrow passage between them.

Mill Brow Mission. *(below left)*

It stood on the site of the present Garden of Remembrance, and came into being through the efforts of Mr. Whiteside. After his sudden death in 1927 no-one would carry on his work, and shortly afterwards the Mission was demolished. It was a 'temporary' structure which lasted 27 years, and was about to be replaced when Mr. Whiteside died. As Councillor Whiteside, he gave many years' service to both Wilmslow Urban District Council and Cheshire County Council, and laid the foundation stone of Wilmslow's first big housing scheme in 1926.

Old Road and River Street, c.1910.

This photograph, clearly shows how the older part of the town is clustered round the Parish Church. The houses in the foreground are in Old Road and River Street, Church Street may be seen above the church roof, with the line of Manchester Road at the left.

Dean Row Chapel. *(right)*

The Chapel was founded in 1688, when the first resident Minister, Eliezer Birch, was appointed. The exact date of the building is uncertain – both 1688 and 1704 are often given – but it certainly existed by 1707 when Birch went to Yarmouth (he later became Minister at Cross Street Chapel, Manchester). Birch was followed by the first Hugh Worthington (1701–1735), followed by his son, another Hugh (1735–1748). The Chapel later declined, both physically and numerically, to be revived under the leadership of the Rev. John Colston of Styal, who conducted the re-opening service on April 23rd, 1845. This postcard view dates from c.1900. In the Chapel yard many of the Greg family have their final resting place.

Dean Row Chapel, Wilmslow.

The Waggon and Horses, on Wilmslow Road near to the junction with Stanley Road. *(right)*

This first appears in directories in the 1870s, though it, too, is shown on the 1844 Tithe Map. It is known to exist at least from 1811. It has been re-built in recent years; this postcard view shows it as it appeared earlier this century.

The Greyhound Inn. *(left)*

It was first listed in directories in 1834, but probably existed some time before that. It is shown on the 1844 Tithe Map of Handforth standing on land owned by John Barratt. The earliest surviving Deed is dated 15th April 1871, by which the property was conveyed from Alfred Barrett to James Bracegirdle for £700. On 25th February 1873 he conveyed it to W. B. Watson for £950. After further changes of ownership it was taken over by Wilson's Brewery in 1966 and by Berni Inns Ltd. in 1978.

In our photograph the arrival of the horse-drawn omnibus is obviously awaited with anticipation.

The Clarion Cycling Club

Following their ejection from temporary premises at Bucklow Hill, the Clarion Cycling Club moved to Handforth, to premises on Outwood Road. They remained in Handforth until 1935, when they moved to Wilmslow, to premises on the site now occupied by the Valley Lodge Hotel. (Wilmslow was vacated in 1951.)

At Handforth, lighting was by carbide lamps. There were Sunday evening concerts, at which poor children from Manchester were entertained. The postmark on the postcard view (right), is October 1909, while that (below right) is postmarked December 1905.

To judge by the Sitting Room members enjoyed a high degree of comfort. The door leads to the Billiard Room, and the portrait on the wall is of Keir Hardie; an unfinished (or interrupted?) game of chess is on the table.

Manchester Road, c.1900
In this view looking north, the trees (left) occupy
the site of the paddock precinct.

St. Chad's Church (Church of England) during construction in 1897.

The little chapel which formerly stood at the junction of Wilmslow Road and Church Road is next to St. Chad's. This chapel is seen to better advantage in the lower photograph taken about the same time. This had been built in 1837 as a Chapel of Ease to Cheadle Parish Church, of which parish Handforth was then a part. The living at Handforth became a Vicarage when the Parish of St. Chad was formed in 1877.

Handforth Station probably looking towards Manchester.

It was taken from below the overline road bridge. Until the newly electrified Manchester–Crewe line opened to passenger traffic in September 1960, the layout at Handforth involved staggered platforms. The up (London-bound) platform was south of the road bridge, with the down (Manchester-bound) platform north of the road bridge; the down platform is seen here. The gang seem to be re-laying the tracks with new sleepers and ballast. The photograph is dated to the period 1900–1914, and shows typical L & N W R timber buildings, signals and lettering.

(Right): The station in the early 1900's.

The Ship Inn, Styal

On 4th September 1900 the owner of the Ship Inn, Styal, Henry P. Greg (nephew of E. H. Greg) displayed the following notice: 'I have given instructions that no one is to be served with more than two glasses of intoxicating liquor at a time'.

For 18 months fever had been present in the village. The Medical Officer was of the opinion that it was brought by strangers. Mr. E. H. Greg's caution was directed against 'the criminal recklessness of visitors from the large towns' who brought the fever with them. 'Many of them were of a drunken, low class, and were most undesirable villagers.' Seen here is the licencee, Mr. Charles Mace, his wife, son Robert A. Mace and Miss Gertrude J. Mace (later Mrs. Middleton), with Robin Hattersley and Miss C. Mace.

Lode Hill House. *(left)*
This house, built for Henry Russell Greg (1832–1894) during the 1860's, has now been demolished.

Norcliffe Hall. *(below)*
Robert Hyde Greg (1795–1875) rented a house in Manchester, but in order to supervise the Quarry Bank Mill more closely, (and also to curtail his expenses!), he decided to live near the Mill. He instructed his architect, Mr. Johnson, not to exceed £2000; Norcliffe Hall was the result. A large neo-Elizabethan house, it was built in 1831 on part of the Oak Estate, and is seen here in 1897.

Farm Fold Cottages, c.1910.

Before Greg arrived in 1784, Styal was a scattered hamlet. Farm Fold was a farmstead, and to accommodate his increasing number of workers, Greg converted the farmstead into dwellings during the 1790s. The farmhouse itself adapted into five dwellings, three were made out of the dairy, and Farm Fold Cottages were converted from a Dutch barn. Does one detect interest, or suspicion, amongst the villagers? The Methodist Chapel, in the background, was converted from a cornstore.

Norcliffe Chapel. *(above)*

The building of the Chapel began in 1822, and it was officially opened early in 1823. It was a private chapel, owned and paid for by Samuel Greg; it remained as a private chapel until 1879. It was originally built for the Baptists; after Greg had provided the Methodists with a chapel (by converting a cornstore, in 1833), Norcliffe became Unitarian. The first (Baptist) Minister was the Rev. Halford Jones, whose stipend (£80 per annum) and house were provided by Greg. The first Unitarian Minister was the Rev. John Colston (1833–1864). The original building had no chancel or porch; these were added during the extensions and alterations carried out in 1867. Greg paid £307.18.0. for the original chapel; his son Robert Hyde Greg paid about £1000 for the 1867 extensions and subsequent decoration! The seated figure is thought to be Edward Hyde Greg (1827–1910).

Styal. *(right)*

These thatched cottages adjoin the Methodist Chapel. Together with other houses in the village, such as Cruck Cottage, Cross Farm and Shaw's Fold, they create an impression of the pre-Greg Hamlet.

Styal 1900. *(above right)*

A turn-of-the-century photograph of the village pond at Styal, showing the lych-gate leading to Norcliffe Chapel, with Oak Cottages behind.

The De Trafford Arms Hotel.

It was serving the needs of the traveller before the railway came and established its own hotel, the Queen's Hotel, in 1844. Andrew Pearson 'could well remember Alderley Edge and neighbourhood before the railway was made . . . the quiet village of Chorley consisted of a few small thatched cottages . . . the old Smithy, and Trafford Arms . . .'.

Wilmslow Carnival, Holly Road, 1910.

This photograph is part of the Alderley contingent to the Wilmslow Carnival. Leading 'John Bull' on 'Moss' is Bill Higginson, whose younger brother Fred, at the left, looks on in admiration.

The Mission and Temperance Hall. *(below)*

It was built in 1878 on London Road as a counter-attraction to the local ale-houses. It is seen here, c.1900, and is now the Church Institute.

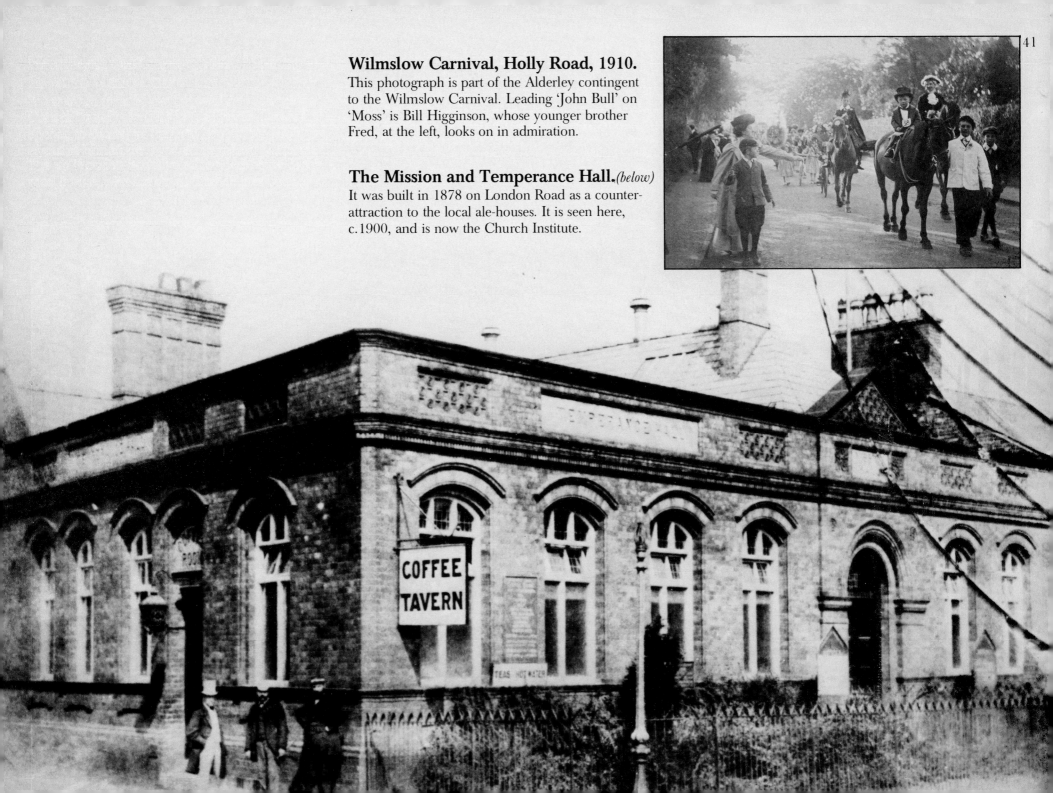

COFFEE TAVERN

Chorley Hall, c.1875

The original part of this moated Hall was built c.1330 by Robert de Chorley. Families associated with the Hall include Honford, Davenport and Stanley; the Stanleys owned it from c.1640 until the estates were sold in 1938. The Tudor wing seen here was added by the Davenports. After serving as a tenanted farmhouse for over 100 years, the Hall is now once again a private residence.

West Mine, Alderley Edge, 1922.

Although mining on Alderley Edge first began over 2000 years ago, what we see today is the result of mining activity only over the last 200 years. Ormerod in 1882 wrote that 'cobalt ore, lead and copper have been got in small quantities'. West Mine was started in 1857 by James Mitchell, who obtained a lease for 20 years from Lord Stanley. This photograph, shows the entrance to West Mine, with its haulage incline.

The Alderley Estate.

The Stanley connection with the Alderley area was severed in 1938 when the estates were sold. Seen here is the stable yard on the estate – one wonders who the distinguished looking gentleman is! The site is now part of the I.C.I. complex.

Nether Alderley Cross. *(above left)*

The Cross in quieter days before the road, the modern A.34, was improved to cope with increasing traffic.

The 'Old Smithy', Bradford Lane. *(above right)*

The 'old Smithy' which Andrew Pearson remembered, photographed in 1896, was a thatched building, situated in Bradford Lane which is actually in Nether Alderley. It was demolished in 1908, and was thought to be about 240 years old. The house opposite (on the left) was occupied by the smith's apprentice. The lane at this point was just wide enough to allow a threshing machine to get past. The house later became the home of the schoolmaster; the school was behind the house, and had been erected by the Hon. Miss Stanley in 1822.

The 'Eagle and Child' at Nether Alderley. *(left)*

It is now a private house, but in former days was a coaching inn; its licence was surrendered about 1870. The name perpetuates a 14th century legend concerning one Sir Thomas Latham, a Stanley forbear.